World War I:
The Great War

Edited by A. J. Scopino, Jr.

Machine gun, set up in a railroad shop in France,
June 7, 1918 (Army photo)

Discovery Enterprises, Ltd.
Carlisle, Massachusetts

© Discovery Enterprises, Ltd., Carlisle, MA 1997

ISBN 1-878668-91-9 paperback edition
Library of Congress Catalog Card Number 96-86739

10   9   8   7   6   5   4   3   2

Printed in the United States of America

Subject Reference Guide:

World War I: The Great War
edited by A.J. Scopino, Jr.

World War I — U.S. History

Woodrow Wilson — U.S. History

Photo Credits:

Cover photo - courtesy of the National Archives

All other illustration and photo credits appear in the text.

Editor's notes regarding the documents:

1. *All original spelling has been retained.*
2. *A full line of dots indicates the deletion of at least an entire paragraph.*

Table of Contents

Navy recruiting poster
(Office of Naval Records and Library)

Introduction

by
A.J. Scopino, Jr.

On Sunday, June 28, 1914, the heir to the Austro-Hungarian throne, Archduke Francis Ferdinand, was assassinated by a Serbian nationalist in the Bosnian capital of Sarajevo. The event set off the worst bloodletting known to humankind at that time. By November of 1918, the First World War, also referred to as "The Great War," would claim some nine million military dead and nearly thirty million wounded, captured, or missing. Another thirty million would be victimized among civilian populations.

Following Ferdinand's assassination, nation after nation lined up to form alliances. The Central Powers included Imperial Germany, the Austro-Hungarian Empire, the Ottoman Empire, and Bulgaria. The Allies included Great Britain, France, Russia, and later, Italy. Amidst the tension, the United States remained on the sidelines transfixed by indecision, neutrality, and indifference. Most Americans were convinced that this war was a European affair, involving an untidy complex of autocrats and their empires. As events unfolded, however, the U.S. would be drawn into the conflict and, by 1918, would help significantly to bring the war to a close.

World War I brought devastation and ruin, in large part due to new weapons technology. The tank not only unleashed firepower but also provided coverage for advancing infantry. The German U-Boat, or submarine, made water travel treacherous, claiming thousands of lives aboard both military vessels and passenger ships. The flamethrower scorched both earth and man. The zeppelin, a large dirigible invented in 1898 by a retired German army officer, and the airplane dropped death from the sky. Chemical warfare, first used systematically by the Germans near Ypres, France on April 22, 1915, shocked, burned, and blistered infantrymen.

World War I also introduced a new military strategy: trench warfare. Long, zigzag lines of burrowed-out earth-works, from which armies could launch attacks and counterattacks, trenches could stretch for miles. Located between opposing trenches was a desolate no-man's land where more conventional weaponry, including the machine gun, reaped its deadly harvest.

While the Central Powers and the Allies were pounding each other in what turned out to be a three-year military stalemate, the United States remained preoccupied with achieving domestic reform. Yet, events arose to shake America from its contented aloofness. First, Germany's invasion of neutral Belgium in 1914 — a key part of the Schlieffen Plan, named after its creator Count Alfred von Schlieffen — shocked the entire world. Second, in 1915, the British passenger liner *Lusitania* was sunk by a German U-Boat, sending over 1,000 people, including 128 Americans, to a watery grave. Third, the uncovering of a secret German telegram proposing a sinister plot between Mexico and Germany to carve up the American Southwest outraged Americans. Fourth, reports, some rumor and others true, circulated calling attention to and condemning German atrocities inflicted on conquered peoples. Americans and many others found this behavior hard, cold, and merciless. Fifth, the resumption of unrestricted submarine warfare by Germany in February of 1917, proved to be the last straw in a series of offenses against the world community. On April 6, Congress gave President Woodrow Wilson the declaration of war against Germany he had asked for four days earlier. For many Americans, here was the opportunity to participate in a war to prevent all future wars and reshape the entire world guided by progressive, liberal, and democratic principles.

While this series of events was unfolding, the United States found itself almost wholly unprepared for war. The world of international bargaining, treaty-making, and empire-building was foreign to the more simple diplomacy that had marked American foreign policy. Yet, within time, the American genius for confronting problems in an efficient, scientific manner took hold and prepared the country for conflict abroad. Soon the nation's technological genius and organizational capability succeeded in bringing needed uniformity to the labor process, standardization to machinery and parts, and greater efficiency to governmental committees, commissions, and boards preparing for war. In addition, some of the most successful and dynamic personalities in the business, professional, labor, and entertainment communities contributed their time and expertise to the war effort.

Following Congress's declaration of April 6, America converted purposefully for war. Industrial managers, directors, engineers, efficiency experts, and other technocrats worked to fashion the new war machine in an efficient and progressive manner. On April 13, the Committee for Public Information (CPI) was formed to promote the war aims of the nation and sway public opinion. In June, the Overman Act set heavy penalties for anyone found interfering with military operations and empowered the post office to withdraw mailing services to anyone advocating treason, insurrection, or resistance to the war effort. The Council of National Defense was established in July and oversaw industrial output in collaboration with the War Industries Board. In August, the Lever Act empowered the Fuel Administration to ration fuel reserves while the Food Administration managed food production and consumption. In October, the War Trade Board assumed control of all exports and imports. The War Finance Board mobilized and allocated needed capital. The War Labor Board secured the cooperation of organized labor, and both groups resolved disputes to keep labor unrest to a minimum. To defend against treason and sedition, Congress passed the Espionage Act and, in 1918, the Sedition Act.

Primed and eager to participate, the first 15,000 troops of what was called the American Expeditionary Force (AEF) arrived in France on June 13, 1917, under the leadership of General John J. ("Black Jack") Pershing. In October, they were joined by another 87,000 troops. America's entry into the war was timely. The Central Powers had overrun most of western Europe and were poised to make another offensive to break a three-year military stalemate. On May 31, 1918, the American Second Division turned back the German advance at Chateau-Thierry and Bellow Wood in France. Between July 15 and August 6, they participated in battles that forced the German retreat from the Marne River. Then, with renewed aggressiveness, the Allies launched a strike that destroyed the German army at St. Mihiel, followed by a massive offensive in the terrain between the Meuse River and the Argonne Forest that ultimately spelled defeat for Imperial Germany.

Soon after, German leader Kaiser Wilhelm II abdicated his throne and fled to Holland. On November 11, 1918, at 11:00 AM, nineteen months after America's declaration of war, an armistice took effect. The Great War had ended. While America suffered less from the war than a host of European nations, it still suffered a great deal. Over 116,000 Americans died — 53,402 in battle — and about 204,000 were wounded. And while men were the principal participants, women went too. Twenty-five thousand American women served overseas during The Great War.

Following the armistice, the Allies' next hurdle was to plan for the restoration of world peace. What followed, however, was a confrontation in ideology. On the one hand, the victorious Allies, eager for the spoils of war, sought to punish the Central Powers. On the other hand, President Wilson's peace plan, called the Fourteen Points, would seek to reintegrate Germany into the world community, establish a mechanism to prevent future conflicts, and urge worldwide cooperation in order to insure the sovereignty of all nations. These bold and visionary principles departed from the self-serving bargaining over territorial rights and possessions, and instead were founded upon a world order imbued with compassion, respect, and mutual understanding. Despite some misgivings within American political circles, Wilson himself went abroad to attend the peace conference.

A confident Wilson returned to the United States and, on June 28, 1919, laid the Treaty of Versailles before Congress, hoping for ratification. Although the President's Fourteen Points were recognizable within it, the American delegation had agreed to many modifications in order to save the one provision Wilson cared about most: a League of Nations. While most of the provisions were acceptable to members of Congress and most Americans, the call for the creation of a League of Nations to monitor world affairs created a tight bottleneck in the drive toward ratification. There arose in the Senate a bipartisan group of "Irreconcilables" who fought American involvement in the League of Nations tooth and nail. Cognizant of the League's invested powers which, in all likelihood, would become a controlling force in world affairs, the "Irreconcilables" feared that alignment with the League would drag the U.S. into further foreign intrigue. The Senate's hardened refusal to commit to further global involvement and Wilson's own stubborn resistance to modifying his terms resulted in nonratification for the treaty and nonparticipation in the League of Nations.

While Congress was rebuking Wilson's peace initiatives, the nation's transition from a wartime to a peacetime economy was fraught with difficulty as well. Labor unrest resulted in some 400 strikes, workers incurred huge wage cuts, inflation skyrocketed, and the cancellation of war orders resulted in mass layoffs.

Economic conditions were highly unsettled. Inspired by the Russian workers' participation in the successful Bolshevik revolution in November of 1917, some Americans, both native-born and foreign-born, began to lay the blame for postwar difficulties at the doorstep of Big Business and American politics. After all, these critics proclaimed, Big Business leaders had profited during the war but did not absorb any of the suffering after the conflict. Politicians, it was argued, protected this arrangement.

For others, however, the attack upon Big Business and American politics was an attack upon the very essence of the American way of life. Furthermore, the emergence of not one, but two, American communist parties in the postwar period — in time they would merge — seemed to confirm in the minds of many that the country indeed faced an internal threat. All forms of political dissent were now regarded as nothing short of treason. Socialists, communists, anarchists, many immigrants, and some labor leaders now found themselves under the shadow of suspicion. What ensued was a suffocating crusade for conformity to American values, institutions, and politics. The country's patriotic fervor, which had reached a boiling point during The Great War, began to spill over in the war's aftermath. The nation's demand for 100% Americanism suddenly erupted into a xenophobic — having an irrational fear of foreigners — crusade.

Reaction to this conspiratorial, yet imaginary, "Red Scare," was an episode in American hysteria and paranoia. Orchestrated under the leadership of J. Edgar Hoover of the U.S. Department of Justice, government officials working in concert with state and local police staged a series of raids in November of 1919 and January of 1920. The dragnet was intended to round up, incarcerate, convict, and rid the country of suspected "radicals" or "reds." What actually occurred was the mass victimization of thousands of innocent immigrants, labor leaders, and political dissenters. Of the thousands arrested during the patriotic frenzy, some 247 "radicals" ultimately were deported. The overwhelming majority of those arrested, with threadbare evidence, were released.

The "war to end all wars" and the postwar concern with global and domestic communism had promoted much change. For one thing, the war gave birth to nine new nations: Poland, Austria, Hungary, Yugoslavia, Czechoslovakia, Latvia, Lithuania, Finland, and Estonia. And though not strictly a new state, Rumania was very much like one because its area and population doubled. Second, in spite of America's determined refusal to commit to the League of Nations, the United States had come of age internationally and was destined to become a leader in world affairs. Third, the war's destructiveness left Europe politically and economically unstable which, in turn, would provide the opening for unscrupulous opportunists to come to power in the 1920s and 1930s. And fourth, the postwar "Red Scare" had sowed the seeds of distrust between America's federal government and its foreign-born population.

In the selections that follow, you will have the opportunity to examine readings that explore America's preparation for, and participation in, The Great War. In addition, you will be able to examine documents concerning the unsettling postwar situation and capture a glimpse of what historians have observed in the era of The Great War.

Preparation for War

In April 1917, President Woodrow Wilson established the Committee on Public Information (CPI) and appointed journalist George Creel as its head. The CPI sought to inform the American public and influence the public consciousness regarding the war. As head of this vast organization, Creel hired writers, university professors, playwrights, essayists, and Hollywood producers to help mold public opinion. It was, according to Creel, a "fight for the minds of men." Under Creel's direction, the CPI published pamphlets, magazines, and produced movies that helped shape public opinion. While maintaining from the beginning that it was not a censorship bureau, the CPI nonetheless, monitored virtually everything the American public read, viewed, and heard about the war. Its messages reached not only the American people but spanned every part of the globe. Turning the war into a patriotic campaign, CPI officials hired Hollywood stars such as Mary Pickford, Douglas Fairbanks, Charlie Chaplin, and Norma Talmadge to help carry the war message at home and overseas. A speakers' bureau, an advertising division, a foreign language section, a newspaper distribution network, and a corps of prominent citizens who delivered four minute speeches were all employed by the CPI. In addition, by asking the American press to adopt voluntary censorship, the agency was able to insure secrecy and thereby promote the safety of American fighting men. In the following excerpt, Creel discusses the creation of the CPI and its singleness of purpose: to mold public opinion.

The CPI: Fighting for the Minds of Men

Source: George Creel, *How We Advertised America* (New York: Harper & Brothers, 1920), pp. 5-8.

There was no part of the great war machinery that we did not touch, no medium of appeal that we did not employ. The printed word, the spoken word, the motion picture, the telegraph, the cable, the wireless, the poster, the sign-board — all these were used in our campaign to make our own people and all other peoples understand the causes that compelled America to take arms. All that was fine and ardent in the civilian population came at our call until more than one hundred and fifty thousand men and women were devoting highly specialized abilities to the work of the Committee, as faithful and devoted in their service as though they wore the khaki.

While America's summons was answered without question by the citizenship as a whole, it is to be remembered that during the three and a half years of our neutrality the land had been torn by a thousand divisive prejudices, stunned by the voices of anger and confusion, and muddled by the pull and haul of opposed interests. These were conditions that could not be permitted to endure. What we had to have was no mere surface unity, but a passionate belief in the justice of America's cause that should weld the people of the United States into one white-hot mass instinct with fraternity, devotion, courage, and deathless determination. The *warwill*, the will-to-win, of a democracy depends upon the degree to which each one of all the people of that democracy can concentrate and consecrate body and soul and spirit in the supreme effort of service and sacrifice. What had to be driven home was that all business was the nation's business, and every task a common task for a single purpose.

Starting with the initial conviction that the war was not the war of an administration, but the war of one hundred million people, believing that public support was a matter of public understanding, we opened up the activities of government to the inspection of the citizenship. A voluntary censorship agreement safeguarded military information of obvious value to the enemy, but in all else the rights of the press were recognized and furthered. Trained men, at the center of effort in every one of the war-making branches of government, reported on progress and achievement, and in no other belligerent nation was there such absolute frankness with respect to every detail of the national war endeavor.

As swiftly as might be, there were put into pamphlet form America's reasons for entering the war, the meaning of America, the nature of our free institutions, our war aims, likewise analyses of the Prussian [the stern, militaristic and autocratic attitudes cultivated by the German military and ruling classes] system, the purposes of the imperial German government, and full exposure of the enemy's misrepresentations, aggressions, and barbarities....

....

The Four Minute Men, an organization that will live in history by reason of its originality and effectiveness, commanded the volunteer services of 75,000 speakers, operating in 5,200 communities, and making a total of 755,190 speeches, every one having the carry of shrapnel.

With the aid of a volunteer staff of several hundred translators, the Committee kept in direct touch with the foreign language press, supplying selected articles designed to combat ignorance and disaffection....

It [the CPI] planned war exhibits for the state fairs of the United States, also a great series of interallied war expositions that brought home to our millions the exact nature of the struggle that was being waged in France....

The Committee mobilized the advertising forces of the country — press, periodical, car, and outdoor — for the patriotic campaign that gave millions of dollars' worth of free space to the national service....

It assembled the artists of America on a volunteer basis for the production of posters, window cards, and similar material of pictorial publicity....

It issued an official daily newspaper, serving every department of government, with a circulation of one hundred thousand copies a day....

It organized a bureau of information for all persons who sought direction in volunteer war-work....

It gathered together the leading novelists, essayists, and publicists of the land, and these men and women, without payment, worked faithfully in the production of brilliant, comprehensive articles that went to the press as syndicate features.

....

Through the medium of the motion picture, America's war progress, as well as the meanings and purposes of democracy, were carried to every community in the United States and to every corner of the world....

Another division prepared and distributed still photographs and stereopticon slides to the press and public....

Only fifty yards from enemy trenches in France, D. W. Griffith (in civilian clothing) directs filming of the movie Hearts of the World. *(1917, War Department)*

An Imaginary Invasion of New Jersey

One of the most effective means of promoting enthusiasm for the war effort was through the recruitment of scholars who contributed to the CPI's pamphlet series. These pamphlets brought home to the American public the barbarity, cunning, and deceitfulness, real and imagined, of Imperial Germany. In March of 1918, John S. P. Tatlock, a professor of English at Stanford University, wrote pamphlet number 15, entitled "Why We Fight Germany," which was based upon an imaginary German invasion of New Jersey. The following passage was one of the most widely quoted.

Source: John S. P. Tatlock, "Why America Fights Germany," Washington: Committee on Public Information (pamphlet), March 1918, quoted in James R. Mock and Cedric Larson, *Words that Won the War: The Story of the Committee on Public Information* (Princeton: Princeton University Press, 1939), pp. 166-67.

Now let us picture what a sudden invasion of the United States by these Germans would mean: sudden, because their settled way is always to attack suddenly. First they set themselves to capture New York City. While their fleet blockades the harbor and shells the city and the forts from far at sea, their troops land somewhere near and advance toward the city in order to cut its rail communications, starve it into surrender and then plunder it. One body of from 50,000 to 100,000 men lands, let us suppose, at Barnegat Bay, New Jersey, and advances without meeting resistance, for the brave but small American army is scattered elsewhere. They pass through Lakewood, a station on the Central Railroad of New Jersey. They first demand wine for the officers and beer for the men. Angered to find that an American town does not contain large quantities of either, they pillage and burn the post office and most of the hotels and stores. Then they demand $1,000,000 from the residents. One feeble old woman tries to conceal $20 which she has been hoarding in her desk drawer; she is taken out and hanged (to save a cartridge). Some of the teachers in two district schools meet a fate which makes them envy her. The Catholic priest and Methodist minister are thrown into a pig-sty, while the German soldiers look on and laugh. Some of the officers quarter themselves in a handsome house on the edge of town, insult the ladies of the family, and destroy and defile the contents of the house. By this time some of the soldiers have managed to get drunk; one of them discharges his gun accidentally, the cry goes up that the residents are firing on the troops, and then hell breaks loose. Robbery, murder and outrage run riot. Fifty leading citizens are lined up against the First National Bank building, and shot. Most of the town and the beautiful pinewoods are burned, and then the troops move on to treat New Brunswick in the same way — if they get there.

Psychological Testing

One of the most ambitious efforts to harness the advances in science in preparation for war occurred in the field of psychological testing. Under the leadership of Robert Mearns Yerkes (1876-1956), a Harvard professor and president of the American Psychological Association (APA), the U.S. Army, in 1917, began testing recruits for proper military placement. At a special APA council meeting in Philadelphia of that year, Yerkes summoned his colleagues to bring the discipline of psychology to the war effort. Measuring mental aptitude, so reasoned Yerkes, would insure the proper placement of recruits in the armed forces and would help win the war. When the war was over, Yerkes and his Psychological Division had tested some 7,000,000 men. The following excerpt indicates the program's subdivisions.

Source: Robert M. Yerkes, "Psychology in Relation to the War," in *American Psychology in Historical Perspective: Addresses of the Presidents of the American Psychological Association, 1892-1977*, Ernest R. Hilgard, ed., (Washington, D.C.: The American Psychological Association, 1978), pp. 194-95. Originally published in *The Psychological Review*, 25, no. 2 (March 1918), pp. 85-115.

MINUTES OF SPECIAL MEETING OF THE COUNCIL OF THE
AMERICAN PSYCHOLOGICAL ASSOCIATION

The president [of the APA] reported his investigations concerning the possibility of the cooperation of psychologists in a scientific capacity in the present emergency....

It was voted that the president be instructed to appoint committees from the membership of the American Psychological Association to render to the government of the United States all possible assistance with psychological problems arising from the present military emergency. The following committees were authorized....

1. Committee on psychological literature relating to military affairs....
   Chairman, Professor Madison Bentley.

2. Committee on the psychological examination of recruits....
   Chairman, Professor Robert M. Yerkes.

3. Committee on the selection of men for tasks requiring special aptitude, as for example various kinds of artillery service, signaling, etc.
   Chairman, Professor E. L. Thorndike.

4. Committee on psychological problems of aviation, including the pertinent literature, the psychological classifications of an aviator, and the relations of these classifications to mechanical problems.
   Chairman, Doctor H. E. Burtt.

5. Committee on psychological problems of incapacity, including those of shell shock, reeducation, etc.
   Chairman, Doctor S. I. Franz.

6. Committee on psychological problems of vocational characteristics and vocational advice. These problems are related to those of reeducation and incapacity.
   Chairman, Professor John B. Watson.

7. Committee on recreation in the army and navy.
   Chairman, Professor George A. Coe.

8. Committee on the pedagogical and psychological problems of military training and discipline.
   Chairman, Professor Charles H. Judd.

9. Committee on the problems of motivation in connection with military activities.
   Chairman, Professor Walter D. Scott.

10. Committee on problems of emotional characteristics, self-control, etc., in their relations to military demands.
    Chairman, Professor Robert S. Woodworth.

11. Committee on acoustic problems and characteristics of the sense of hearing in relation to military service....
    Chairman, Professor Carl E. Seashore.

12. Committee on problems of vision which have military significance.
    Chairman, Professor Raymond Dodge.

It was voted that, in order to provide the necessary funds for the development of the plans for national service, the council instruct the president of the association to appoint a special finance committee ...empowered to raise and disburse a special fund....

It was moved and seconded that the secretary be instructed to formulate a letter to the members of the association describing the action of the council at this special meeting, in the hope that the members will communicate with the president concerning the best methods of offering their own resources and the resources of their laboratories to the government.

The council made certain suggestions to the president concerning the presentation to the proper government authorities of a plan for the psychological examination of recruits, and authorized the president to proceed with such presentation.

HERBERT S. LANGFELD,
Secretary, American Psychological Association.

Test 11

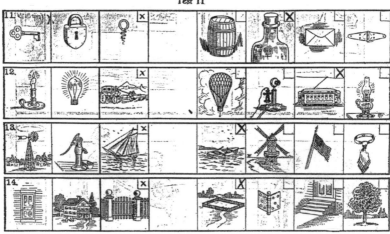

Sample problems from Test 11, Analogies

Engine room of an oil-burning German submarine. (War Department)

The Zimmermann Telegram

On November 12, 1916, German diplomat Arthur Zimmermann — soon to become Foreign Minister — sent a mysterious coded message, via telegram, to the German Minister to Mexico, von Eckhardt. Intercepted and decoded by British cryptographers, the message was startling. Anticipating U.S. entry into the war on the Allied side, Imperial Germany invited Mexico to join the Central Powers. In return for its efforts toward winning the war, Germany promised to reward Mexico with the return of lands previously lost to the United States, namely, Arizona, New Mexico, and Texas. Shown to President Wilson in late February of 1917, the document's existence was revealed in the American press on March 1. This now notorious "Zimmermann Telegram" outraged Americans and led to a new sentiment that helped to dissolve U.S. neutrality, indifference, and indecision. On April 6, 1917, Congress declared war on Germany. Presented on pages 20 and 21 are the telegram in code and the decoded text from the files of the National Archives.

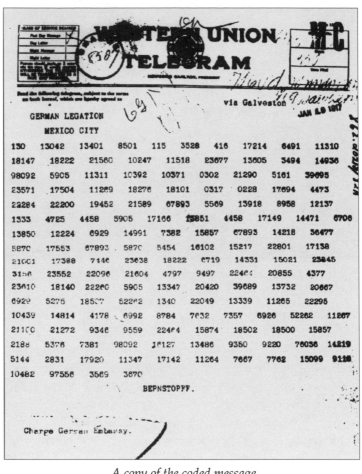

WESTERN UNION TELEGRAM									

via Galveston   JAN 19 1917

GERMAN LEGATION

MEXICO CITY

130	13042	13401	8501	115	3528	416	17214	6491	11310
18147	18222	21560	10247	11518	23677	13605	3494	14936	
98092	5905	11311	10392	10371	0302	21290	5161	39695	
23571	17504	11269	18276	18101	0317	0228	17694	4473	
22284	22200	19452	21589	67893	5569	13918	8958	12137	
1333	4725	4458	5905	17166	13851	4458	17149	14471	6706
13850	12224	6929	14991	7382	15857	67893	14218	36477	
5870	17553	67893	5870	5454	16102	15217	22801	17138	
21001	17388	7446	23638	18222	6719	14331	15021	23845	
3156	23552	22096	21604	4797	9497	22464	20855	4377	
23610	18140	22260	5905	13347	20420	39689	13732	20667	
6929	5275	18507	52262	1340	22049	13339	11265	22295	
10439	14814	4178	6992	8784	7632	7357	6926	52262	11267
21100	21272	9346	9559	22464	15874	18502	18500	15857	
2188	5376	7381	98092	16127	13486	9350	9220	76036	14219
5144	2831	17920	11347	17142	11264	7667	7762	15099	9110
10482	97556	3569	3670						

BEPNSTOPFF.

Charge German Embassy.

A copy of the coded message

FROM 2nd from London # 5747.

"We intend to begin on the first of February
unrestricted submarine warfare. We shall endeavor
in spite of this to keep the United States of
america neutral. In the event of this not succeed-
ing, we make Mexico a proposal of alliance on the
following basis: make war together, make peace
together, generous financial support and an understanding on our part that Mexico is to reconquer
the lost territory in Texas, New Mexico, and
arizona. The settlement in detail is left to you.
You will inform the President of the above most
secretly as soon as the outbreak of war with the
United States of America is certain and add the
suggestion that he should, on his own initiative,
invite Japan to immediate adherence and at the same
time mediate between Japan and ourselves. Please
call the President's attention to the fact that
the ruthless employment of our submarines now
offers the prospect of compelling England in a
few months to make peace." Signed, ZIMMERMANN.

A copy of the decoded message

Warfare against Mankind

Amidst international protest, Imperial Germany halted its policy of unrestricted submarine warfare in April of 1916. As the war intensified, however, Germany renewed its deadly policy on February 1, 1917. Once again, all ships, including commercial vessels and passenger liners of both neutral and belligerent nations making their way to or from ports hostile to Germany, would be subject to submarine attack. Incensed at this development, President Wilson called a Joint Session of Congress on April 2, 1917, advised that Germany's action was, in essence, a declaration of war against the United States, and called upon Congress to "accept the status of belligerent."

Source: 65 Congress, 1 Session, Senate Document No. 5, quoted in *1916-1918: World War and Prosperity*, vol. 14 of *The Annals of America* (Chicago and other cities: Encyclopedia Britannica, Inc., 1968), pp. 77-82.

I have called the Congress into extraordinary session because there are serious, very serious, choices of policy to be made, and made immediately, which it was neither right nor constitutionally permissible that I should assume the responsibility of making.

On the 3rd of February last, I officially laid before you the extraordinary announcement of the Imperial German government that on and after the 1st day of February it was its purpose to put aside all restraints of law or of humanity and use its submarines to sink every vessel that sought to approach either the ports of Great Britain and Ireland or the western coasts of Europe or any of the ports controlled by the enemies of Germany within the Mediterranean.

The present German submarine warfare against commerce is a warfare against mankind. It is a war against all nations....The challenge is to all mankind.

Each nation must decide for itself how it will meet it. The choice we make for ourselves must be made with a moderation of counsel and a temperateness of judgment befitting our character and our motives as a nation....

When I addressed the Congress on the 26th of February last, I thought that it would suffice to assert our neutral rights with arms, our right to use the seas against unlawful interference, our right to keep our people safe against unlawful,violence. But armed neutrality, it now appears, is impracticable....

With a profound sense of the solemn and even tragical character of the step I am taking and of the grave responsibilities which it involves, but in unhesitating obedience to what I deem my constitutional duty, I advise that the Congress declare the recent course of the Imperial German Government to be in fact nothing less than war against the government and people of the United States; that it formally accept the status of belligerent which has thus been thrust upon it; and that it take immediate steps, not only to put the country in a more thorough state of defense but also to exert all its power and employ all its resources to bring the government of the German Empire to terms and end the war.

We have no quarrel with the German people. We have no feeling toward them but one of sympathy and friendship. It was not upon their impulse that their government acted in entering this war. It was not with their previous knowledge or approval. It was a war determined upon as wars used to be determined upon in the old, unhappy days when peoples were nowhere consulted by their rulers and wars were provoked and waged in the interest of dynasties or of little groups of ambitious men who were accustomed to use their fellowmen as pawns and tools.

...[We have been convinced] at last that that government entertains no real friendship for us and means to act against our peace and security at its convenience. That it means to stir up enemies against us at our very doors the intercepted note to the German minister at Mexico City is eloquent evidence.

We are accepting this challenge of hostile purpose because we know that in such a government, following such methods, we can never have

23

a friend; and that in the presence of its organized power, always lying in wait to accomplish we know not what purpose, there can be no assured security for the democratic governments of the world....

The world must be made safe for democracy. Its peace must be planted upon the tested foundations of political liberty. We have no selfish ends to serve. We desire no conquest, no dominion. We seek no indemnities for ourselves, no material compensation for the sacrifices we shall freely make. We are but one of the champions of the rights of mankind. We shall be satisfied when those rights have been made as secure as the faith and the freedom of nations can make them.

....

It is a distressing and oppressive duty, gentlemen of the Congress, which I have performed in thus addressing you. There are, it may be, many months of fiery trial and sacrifice ahead of us. It is a fearful thing to lead this great peaceful people into war, into the most terrible and disastrous of all wars, civilization itself seeming to be in the balance. But the right is more precious than peace, and we shall fight for the things which we have always carried nearest our hearts — for democracy, for the right of those who submit to authority to have a voice in their own governments, for the rights and liberties of small nations, for a universal dominion of right by such a concert of free peoples as shall bring peace and safety to all nations and make the world itself at last free.

To such a task we can dedicate our lives and our fortunes, everything that we are and everything that we have, with the pride of those who know that the day has come when America is privileged to spend her blood and her might for the principles that gave her birth and happiness and the peace which she has treasured. God helping her, she can do no other.

Radical Pacifism

As the United States prepared for war, not all Americans were convinced that engaging in hostilities was the proper response to events in Europe. A small but vocal group of clergy adopted a pacifist stand opposing the war for religious, social, or economic reasons. Inspired by the progressive and scientific approach to confronting the problems of his era, John Haynes Holmes, a Unitarian clergyman, located the root of war in economic competition that pitted nation against nation. Once this ruthless competition was abandoned, Holmes argued, militarism and war would also cease. In 1916, he put forth a statement on "radical pacifism," a position which condemned militarism and economic competition. To the end of the war Holmes would encourage Americans to remain a "people of ideas" and not sacrifice their idealism and democratic principles to those who would lead the nation "into the treacherous ways of blood and iron." The following excerpt embodies his position on "radical pacifism."

Source: John Haynes Holmes, *New Wars for Old: Being a Statement of Radical Pacifism in Terms of Force Versus Non-Resistance, with Special Reference to the Facts and Problems of the Great War* (New York: Dodd, Mead and Company, 1916), pp. 345-48.

In these two great ideas of brotherhood and democracy, is the essence of American life. This is what America means to-day, as Greece yesterday meant beauty and Rome law. And just here in this spiritual idea of nationality, do we find the supreme and unanswerable vindication of the men who would save America at this time from militarism and the huge armaments which militarism would build. Of course, if you have no higher conception of America than a stretch of land, comprising forty-eight states, three-and-a-half million square miles of territory, one hundred millions of inhabitants, and no higher conception of patriotism than a frenzied passion to make the inhabitants of this particular political division of the earth's surface the dominant people of the world, then you had better build as many dreadnaughts and train as many soldiers as you can, for these weapons can alone avail you anything in this realm of sheer materialism. But if you look upon America as a great ideal of the spirit, independent of territory and population and wealth, then all such things as armies and navies become matters of supreme indifference. For the spirit is impregnable to all the attacks that the hand of man can bring against it. What if the soldiers of another nation should occupy our territory, seize our ports, capture our cities, occupy our strongholds, levy tribute upon our citizens? What if Germany came here today as she came to Belgium yesterday! Would she not find it as impossible to conquer "the soul of America" as she has already found it impossible to conquer the soul of Belgium? No conqueror that has ever lived could destroy the sense of brotherhood that is at the heart of our American life: no sword that was ever forged could smite the love of democracy which is the impulse of our civilization. A free people would still be free, even though in chains — and a valiant spirit still survive, even the hour of death. Nay, we will not only not be conquered, but we will ourselves be conquerors in this higher realm of the spirit. Let our enemies come against us with sword and shield and trumpet, and we will meet them with our faith in brotherhood and democracy. And, behold, in the very process of this conquest, they will themselves be conquered! America will conquer the thousands who come in arms against her, as she has already conquered the millions who have sought her shores in peace!

To all such attacks as these, the soul of America is impregnable. But there is another kind of attack, which may well be feared by all those who love this nation not for what she has, but for what she is. I refer to the attack not upon her soil but upon her soul — an attack which is now being conducted all along the line by those who, for the reasons which I have described, would have America abandon her priceless ideals of brotherhood and democracy, and follow the melancholy example of the great empires of history. Why worry about the enemies who may be lying in wait against our country on some far horizon of the sea, when enemies much more serious are lying in wait against her right here within her borders? Why worry about the armies and dreadnaughts that may be marshalled against her territory in Germany or Japan, when lies and deceits are even now being marshalled against her soul in Washington...? Our real foes are of our own household —

those men who, from motives however worldly, would lead America out of the trodden paths of fraternity and peace, into the treacherous ways of blood and iron. Once let the policy of armaments get fastened upon this Republic, and our mission as a nation is at an end. No longer shall we be a people of ideas. On the contrary, we shall be a people of wealth, power, dominion, glory — a people who measure their greatness by the territory they occupy or the trade they own, and not by the ideals of the spirit which they serve. In becoming an empire we shall lose that brotherhood which has long been the hope of a disordered world. In becoming a "great power" we shall sacrifice that democracy which long has been the open door of opportunity to mankind. In gaining the whole world, we shall lose our own soul — die as Athens died, Rome died, Spain died! Here is a conquest to be feared in very earnest — a conquest beside which the bombardment of cities and the ravaging of territory are as nothing. If I had to choose between having America's soil over-run from end to end by the triumphant legions of Von Hindenburg, and having her soil untouched by the foot of the invader, but her soul at the same time surrendered to the gospel of Treitschke and Bernhardi, I would unhesitatingly choose the former fate. For nothing is lost, if the soul is safe; and nothing is safe, if the soul is lost. And it is just because our militarists, on the specious plea of saving our shores from invasion, are doing nothing more nor less than opening the soul of America to a peril of conquest of this kind, that, in spite of their sincerity, they are to be so greatly feared....

To keep America faithful to her ideals — to help her at this crisis of temptation, to preserve her soul inviolate – – this is the highest duty of the present hour. And this duty has a purpose which far transcends the selfish interests of the American people themselves. For why is it the duty of America to preserve her ideals, if not that she may transmit these ideals to the world?...

Hoover's Observations of German Rule

After neutral Belgium was overrun by Germany at the outset of the war, Herbert Clark Hoover, a Stanford-trained engineer, became head of the Commission for Relief in Belgium. With America's entry into the war, Hoover returned home and, at President Wilson's invitation, became leader of the newly-created Food Administration, a government agency that managed food supplies, prices, and rationing during hostilities. The reading that follows is a letter that Hoover had sent to the CPI in September of 1917. Accounts such as these helped galvanize American distrust and dislike of Imperial Germany.

Source: Dana C. Munro, ed., *German War Practices* (Washington: The Committee on Public Information, 1917), pp. 81-82.

September, 1917

I have been often called upon for a statement of my observation of German rule in Belgium and Northern France.

I have neither the desire nor the adequate pen to picture the scenes which have heated my blood through the two and a half years that I have spent in work for the relief of these 10,000,000 people.

The sight of the destroyed homes and cities, the widowed and fatherless, the destitute, the physical misery of a people but partially nourished at best, the deportation of men by tens of thousands to slavery in German mines and factories, the execution of men and women for paltry effusions of their loyalty to their country, the sacking of every resource through financial robbery, the battening of armies on the slender produce of the country, the denudation of the country of cattle, horses, and textiles; all these things we had to witness, dumb to help other than by protest and sympathy, during this long and terrible time — and still these are not the events of battle heat, but the effects of a grinding heel of a race demanding the mastership of the world.

All these things are well known to the world — but what can never be known is the dumb agony of the people, the expressionless faces of millions whose souls have passed the whole gamut of emotions. And why? Because these, a free and democratic people, dared to plunge their bodies before the march of autocracy.

I myself believe that if we do not fight and fight now, all these things are possible to us — but even should the broad Atlantic prove our present defender, there is still Belgium. Is it worth while for us to live in a world where this free and unoffending people is to be trampled into the earth and to raise no sword in protest?

Herbert Hoover

Conflict

Alan Seeger was born in New York on June 22, 1888. Much-traveled, a writer of poetry, and a Harvard graduate (class of 1910), Seeger became enamored with France and its culture. With the outbreak of hostilities in 1914, and France threatened with invasion, Seeger was one of a small number of Americans who volunteered for service in the French Foreign Legion in defense of the country he came to love. He was a romantic, an idealist, and a determined French partisan, and in his diary, letters, and poems, published post-humously, he captures the essence of dedication to a cause. In the first selection, excerpted from a letter to the New York Sun *in December of 1914, Seeger discusses life in the trenches as experienced by what he calls the "common soldier." In "I Have a Rendevouz with Death," Seeger reveals his unwillingness to shirk what he sees as his duty to serve France. Alan Seeger was killed in July of 1916, near the French village of Belloy-en-Santerre, in an assault upon a German trench.*

Life in the Trenches

Source: Alan Seeger, *Letters and Diary of Alan Seeger* (New York: Charles Scribners Sons, 1917), pp. 28-30.

True, occasionally a violent fusillade to the right or left of us shows that attacks are being made and at any moment are likely to be made, but these are only struggles for position, and in general the infantry on the centre are being utilized only to support the long line of batteries harrying each other at short distances across field and forest and vineyard.

This style of warfare is extremely modern and for the artillerymen is doubtless very interesting, but for the common soldier it is anything but romantic. His role is simply to dig himself a hole in the ground and to keep hidden in it as tightly as possible. Continually under the fire of the opposing batteries, he is yet never allowed to get a glimpse of the enemy. Exposed to all the dangers of war, but with none of its enthusiasms or splendid *elan*, [French for spirit and vigor] he is condemned to sit like an animal in its burrow and hear the shells whistle over his head and to take their little daily toll from his comrades.

Allied and German planes engage in dogfight.
(Library of Congress)

The winter morning dawns with the gray skies and the hoar frost on the fields. His feet are numb, his canteen frozen, but he is not allowed to make a fire. The winter night falls, with its prospect of sentry duty and the continual apprehension of the hurried call to arms; he is not even permitted to light a candle, but must fold himself in his blanket and lie down cramped in the dirty straw to sleep as best he may. How different from the popular notion of the evening campfire, the songs and good cheer.

Cramped quarters breed ill temper and disputes. The impossibility of the simplest kind of personal cleanliness makes vermin a universal ill, against which there is no remedy. Cold, dirt, discomfort, are the ever present conditions, and the soldier's life comes to mean to him simply the test of the most misery that the human organism can support. He longs for an attack, anything for a little freedom and function for body and soul.

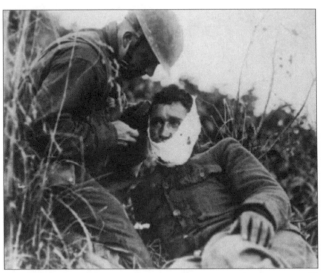

Wounded soldier from the 110th Regiment Infantry on the front in France receives first aid.
(Army photo)

"I Have a Rendevouz with Death"

Source: Alan Seeger, *Poems By Alan Seeger* (New York: Charles Scribners Son's, 1920), p. 144.

I have a rendevouz with Death
At some disputed barricade,
When Spring comes back with rustling shade
And apple-blossoms fill the air —
I have a rendevouz with Death
When Spring brings back blue days and fair.

It may be he shall take my hand
And lead me into his dark land
And close my eyes and quench my breath —
It may be I shall pass him still.
On some scarred slope of battered hill,
When Spring comes round his year
And the first meadow-flowers appear.

God knows "twere better to be deep
Pillowed in silk and scented down,
Where Love throbs out in blissful sleep,
Pulse nigh to pulse, and breath to breath,
Where hushed awakenings are dear....
But I've a rendevouz with Death
At midnight in some flaming town,
When Spring trips north again this year,
And I to my pledged word am true,
I shall not fail that rendevouz.

Animal Heroes

Shortly after the war, writer and photographer E. H. Baynes spent nine months traveling through western Europe and the Middle East gathering information on animals' contributions to victory. Baynes found that many kinds played a vital, if often overlooked, role in the war effort. Horses, mules, oxen, camels, and donkeys transported equipment, supplies, and troops. Dogs stood guard for prisoners of war and served as guides for those blinded in battle. Pigeons and dogs carried messages over hostile territory. Like the men they served, animals were exposed to danger and destruction. Baynes estimated that some 8,000,000 horses alone perished during World War I. In this excerpt, he discusses the suffering animals experienced during chemical warfare attacks.

Source: Ernest Harold Baynes, *Animal Heroes of the Great War* (New York: The Macmillan Company, 1926), pp. 237-40.

Mustard gas produced a set of injuries entirely different, such as lesions of the skin and mucous membrane. Animals driven through territory bombarded by gas developed burns on the hoofs, on sweaty portions of their bodies, and wherever the harness rubbed. The burns were generally superficial, but they were liable to become seriously complicated by secondary infections, which, taking the form of bronchopneumonia, were a common cause of death. Mustard gas evaporated slowly and its evil effects persisted long after a bombardment. Even after two days animals were affected by eating contaminated herbage.

Protection against mustard gas was gained in some degree by careful disinfection after a bombardment of the ground, and of all contaminated harness and other material. Exposed horses were taken in hand as soon as possible and sponged with soap and hot water.

Fortunately, horses are far less sensitive than men to the effects of toxic gases. This is because of the length of their upper respiratory tracts, where contaminated air comes in contact with a large total area of moist surface. Animal losses from exposure to waves of gaseous chlorine, with or without other toxic products were inconsiderable. A

34

bombardment of average intensity generally reaped but a small harvest among animals, partly because they were not very susceptible to it and partly because they were somewhat sheltered by their distance behind the front. However, it happened many times that intensive bombardment with special shells put large numbers of animals out of action.

It was a constant struggle to get the mules through the mud.
(September 13, 1918, Army photo)

The death of animals, although guarded against for the animals' sake, was less serious than the handicap to the fighting line through disablement of animals serving it. Often, such disablement brought German victory measurably closer. Take the gas attack at Bois Maretz [France]: Three horse-drawn wagons loaded with gas masks for the front line troops were being hurried forward in response to urgent signals; they had to pass through a zone of toxic bombardment, and every horse died before the destination was reached. In a similar attack at Craonne [France] in April, 1917, a battery of trench mortars lost twelve out of its thirteen horses.

Casualties like these...established the necessity of protective appliances for the animals that would permit them to go on with their work. Collective measures for group protection were not difficult; ground could be disinfected, bivouacs and stables could be located at points sheltered from gas. Stables could be well ventilated, lest the ammonia given off by the animal discharges should combine with chlorine to produce chloramine, a dangerously toxic product. Stable exits could be closed by cloths water-proofed with boiled linseed oil; spraying could always be resorted to. Open fires to reduce penetration of a toxic atmosphere, however, were found to be untrustworthy.

The urgent employment of animals was the bringing up of supplies, which was prevented once the animals' organs of respiration were affected by toxic gases. The protection of the respiratory system was of primary importance, and numberless devices were experimented with, some with a measure of success, though most of them had serious drawbacks. Horses at rest could be protected easily; horses at work presented a hard problem. Almost any mask was liable to make breathing difficult. Hard-working animals, becoming winded, could not breathe in them at all. They became excited, and if the mask was not removed asphyxiation was likely to follow.

The best types of mask finally evolved were designed to be worn over the bridle, which aided in preventing pressure to the mask against the nostrils. Horses could breathe more easily in these than any other. Most horses submitted quickly to the mask and made the best of it...their equine intelligence apparently grasping the fact that man, whom they served, was doing his best to serve them.

An Attaché's Notebook

When the war broke out, Eric Fisher Wood, an American architectural student at the École des Beaux-Arts in Paris, was working as an attaché for the American Embassy. Between September and November of 1914, he made four trips to the front and viewed the carnage unleashed at the battle of the Marne. In the following excerpt, Wood describes the destructive power of The Great War.

Source: Eric Fisher Wood, *The Note-Book of an Attaché: Seven Months in the War Zone* (New York: The Century Company, 1915), pp. 98-102.

We tried to comprehend the battle as a whole by studying a great many fields, any one of which would a few years ago have been considered an entire battle in itself. The dead were scattered far and wide; and in the fields and among the grain-stacks the wounded cried out their piteous faint appeals. Little groups of German stragglers were hiding in the forests, and squads of alert French soldiers hunted them down, beating through the cover as eager setter dogs search for grouse. In one field of about six acres lay nine hundred German dead and wounded; across another, where a close-action fight had raged, two hundred French and Germans lay mixed together, all mashed and ripped. Here was the curious sight of a German and Frenchman lying face to face, both dead, and each one transfixed by the other's bayonet.

The very birds of the air and the beasts of the field lay dead and rotting amid the general destruction. We saw feathers and bits of chickens and halves of cows. On one occasion Hall [Wood's driver throughout his coverage of the war] maintained that "it" had been a cow, while I thought "it" was a horse, and no piece large enough for certain identification could be found. Of some of the villages which had been peaceful and beautiful a week ago, there remained now only chimneys, ashes, and bits of walls rising from smouldering gray debris. A French village wrecked by battle looks very much wrecked indeed, in contrast with its habitual orderly and toy-like appearance.

I was not so horrified in viewing these ghastly sights as I had expected, because I could not put from me a sense of their unreality. The human mind is incapable of comprehending to the full such terrible happenings. One kept endlessly saying to oneself: "Can all this which we are seeing really have taken place in this once quiet French country-side, almost within the suburbs of Paris? It seems impossible — unbelievable!"

In the little upland village of Clamanges was a field hospital which had been established by the Germans when they first occupied the place on the night of September 7th. They had held it until their retreat on the 10th, when their retirement was so precipitate that they had been unable to take with them their wounded.

In this war it is the custom to convert the village churches into hospitals. The chairs and benches are thrown out into the graveyard and the floor is covered with straw upon which the wounded are laid in long rows extending the length of the nave. The altar is converted into the pharmacist's headquarters and bottles and medicaments are piled thereon, while bandages, for want of room, are sometimes hung upon the statue of the Virgin, who has, in this unique service, an air of sublime and compassionate contentment. An operating room is usually established in the vestry or in the Parish Room and a Red Cross flag is hung from the steeple. Any shell holes in the roofs and walls are stopped with sections of tenting. As we approached Clamanges, we detected a sickening, subtle, sweetish odor which crept stealthily to us through the air and filled us with an insinuating disgust. The Colonel said simply, "That is gangrene."

The streets of the village were muddy and littered, and there were innumerable ominous flies everywhere. The town was crammed with German wounded. In the church long rows of them, touching feet to head and arm to arm, so that the attendants had to step gingerly between as they made their slow way about. The neighboring peasant houses were packed full with the overflow. In the halls lay the bodies of men who had died of gangrene, and as no one had time to attend to the dead, the piles of them grew and increased. We were told that there were thirteen hundred wounded in the village, among whom labored sixty attendants. They were all severely wounded, since the

Germans had dragged with them all their slightly wounded, these being good assets.

What had once been a little rose garden was piled high with a gigantic heap of bloody accoutrements which had been taken from wounded men as they were brought in. Under a tree in a corner of the church-yard a surgeon had set up a big kitchen table which he used for opera-tions; the ground underneath was black and caked. In a near by corner of the church walls was a great pile of boots and stained clothes which had been cut from shattered limbs, and I expect one might have dis-covered even more ghastly objects had one ventured to turn over the rags. The attendants were nearly all French, although two German doctors and several German orderlies had stayed behind with their wounded. All worked heroically to cope with their great task.

The women of France kept agricultural produce available for the troops by using themselves as beasts of burden to pull heavy farm equipment.
(Food Administration photo)

The American Negro in the War

When America entered the war, African-Americans answered the call to arms in large numbers. Over 400,000 served in the U.S. Army and many engaged in combat in Europe. Their courage and valor earned them praise from ally and enemy alike. Still, the ever-present issue of race locked black soldiers into segregated units. White officers mistreated them, and some civilians even objected to having them train in camps located nearby. On October 5, 1917, Emmett J. Scott, former secretary to black leader Booker T. Washington, was appointed Special Assistant for Negro Affairs to the Secretary of War. With convenient access to war documents, Scott was able to publish in 1919 the history from which the excerpt below was taken. While filled with noble exploits of African-Americans on the battlefield and on the homefront, it also documents their hardships. Here Scott summarizes the unfair treatment they received.

Source: Emmett J. Scott, *Scott's Official History of the American Negro in the World War* (New York: Arno Press, 1969), pp. 428-30. Several editions were published in 1919, including one by Homewood Press and one by Victory Publishing Company.

In the beginning of the draft, when men were being first called to the colors, there was much apprehension among Negroes as to whether they would be treated as other soldiers in the camps. The manifest discrimination practiced by various Local Draft Boards against the Negro men in many sections under the Selective Service Law, together with the almost certain knowledge that they would, in many circumstances, be placed under the command of white officers, some of whom at least, it was feared, would not entertain a friendly and sympathetic attitude toward them, increased their apprehension. The fact that three Local Draft Boards were peremptorily ordered removed by the Secretary of State because of their flagrant injustice to Negro draftees is in itself a "straw" which shows that the wind was blowing in the wrong direction. Instances upon instances can be cited to show that the Negro did not get a "square deal" in the draft; in many sections he contributed many more than his quota; and in defiance of both the spirit and letter of the draft law, Negro married men with large families to support were impressed into military service regardless of their protests and appeals, and their wives, children, and dependents suffered un-called-for hardships. Local Draft Boards, in almost every instance composed exclusively of white men, were in a position, if so inclined, to show favoritism to men of their own race; the official figures of the draft reveal the fact that in many sections of the country exemptions were granted white men who were single with practically no dependents, while Negroes were conscripted into service regardless of their urgent need in Agriculture or the essential industries, and without considering their family relations or obligations.

The draft lottery (National Archives)

Would it not have been eminently just and fair, and more in line with the spirit of the American Constitution, to have granted the Negro his rightful quota of representation on Local Draft Boards and District Boards of Appeal which have passed upon matters of such vital consequence to him? This is a question which should be answered in the affirmative.

The Negro was willing to do his full share of the fighting, but the official record shows that he was called upon to do more than his share under the Draft Law, for, although constituting 10.7 percent of the total population of the United States, he contributed 13.08 per cent of the total colored and white inductions from June 5, 1917, to November 11, 1918. He had practically no representation upon the Draft Boards which passed upon his appeals — an arrangement which was wholly at variance with the theory of American institutions.

To catalogue or specify all of the complaints that have come to the War Department, that have been published in the Negro press, and that have been contained in letters written to the relatives of Negro soldiers with reference to unfair treatment accorded them would be an almost endless task, and would consume far more space than can possibly be allotted in this volume, but a few typical ones are given herein. They include charges of harsh and even brutal treatment by some of their commanding officers and especially by white "noncoms" [low-ranking officers] who were placed over them.

A column of black infantrymen marches toward the front northwest of Verdun, France, in October 1918. (National Archives)

Colored Americans have deeply resented the "table of organization" [Table of organization simply refers to the bureaucratic pecking order where whites dominated in positions of power and authority} which denied colored soldiers the privilege of serving as non-commissioned officers over men of their own race. It was further alleged...that white officers and white "noncoms" required of them unusually hard tasks under the most trying circumstances and frequently cursed them, beat them, domineered over them as if they were "slaves" instead of fellows in a common cause....A lack of medical care and proper nursing, inferior food, clothing, and sleeping accommodations were also alleged. In one camp in Virginia it was actually found that no adequate facilities whatsoever had been provided for Negro soldiers who were sick; they were huddled together, fourteen, sixteen and eighteen in one tent, without any wooden floors in the tents, although it was in the midst of the cold winter of 1917, and with practically no hospital accommodations.

Similar disparities between accommodations provided for white and colored soldiers occurred at other camps and occasioned considerable complaint. Perhaps,...nothing contributed so much to friction in the Army as did the assignment of, and the wrongful attitude manifested by white "non-coms" who served in connection with Negro troops.

Freedom of Expression

In 1917, Charles T. Schenck, general secretary of the Socialist Party in America, began circulating leaflets condemning the draft and urging men to ignore the appeal to arms. Schenck and others were arrested and charged with violating the Espionage Act of 1917 which prohibited any obstruction of the war effort. What resulted was the landmark case Schenck v. United States *(1919) involving the sensitive issue of freedom of expression. Supreme Court Justice Oliver Wendell Holmes, who wrote the opinion, argued that free speech in particular circumstances, such as war, would not be protected when it presented a "clear and present danger" to the nation's safety. Schenck's conviction was upheld by a unanimous Court.*

Source: Alfred Lief, ed., *The Dissenting Opinions of Mr. Justice Holmes* (New York: The Vanguard Press, 1929), pp. 231-34.

This is an indictment in three counts. The first charges a conspiracy to violate the Espionage Act of June 15, 1917...by causing and attempting to cause insubordination...and to obstruct the recruiting and enlistment service of the United States, when the United States was at war with the German Empire....

The second count alleges a conspiracy to commit an offense against the United States, to-wit, to use the mails for transmission of matter declared to be non-mailable by Title XII,...of the Act of June 15, 1917 ....The third count charges an unlawful use of the mails for the transmission of the same matter and otherwise as above.

....

Schenck personally attended to the printing. On August 20 the [Socialist Party] general secretary's report said, "Obtained new leaflets from printer and started work addressing envelopes,"...and there was a resolve that Comrade Schenck be allowed $125 for sending leaflets through the mail...copies were proved to have been sent through the mails to drafted men. Without going into confirmatory details that were proved, no reasonable man could doubt that the defendant Schenck was largely instrumental in sending the circulars about.

....

The document in question...intimated that conscription was despotism in its worst form and a monstrous wrong against humanity in the interest of Wall Street's chosen few....

It described the arguments [for conscription]...as coming from cunning politicians and a mercenary capitalist press,....

We admit that in many places and in ordinary times the defendants in saying all that was said in the circular would have been within their constitutional rights. But the character of every act depends upon the circumstances in which it is done....The most stringent protection of free speech would not protect a man in falsely shouting fire in a threater and causing a panic. It does not even protect a man from an injunction against uttering words that may have all the effect of force.

...The question in every case is whether the words used are used in such circumstances and are of such a nature as to create a clear and present danger that they will bring about the substantive evils that Congress has a right to prevent. It is a question of proximity and degree.

When a nation is at war many things that might be said in time of peace are such a hindrance to its effort that their utterance will not be endured so long as men fight and that no court could regard them as protected by any constitutional right....

The Postwar Struggle

With victory achieved, the Allied leaders met early in 1919 to hammer out a peace treaty. But while America's Allies sought to restore world peace, they also were determined to inflict a punitive settlement on Germany by seizing her African colonies, setting restrictions upon her armed forces, imposing an enormous reparations bill, and tagging her with war guilt. At the same time, however, Woodrow Wilson was framing a different set of proposals. Visionary, idealistic, and inspired by nearly two decades of progressive thought and action in America, Wilson's "Fourteen Points," as the plan came to be known, embodied a blueprint for a peaceful future, one that was not based on empires and autocracy, but upon open discussion, cooperation, and respect for the sovereignty of all nations. The principles of the Fourteen Points are listed below.

The Fourteen Points

Source: Albert Shaw, ed., *President Wilson's State Papers and Addresses* (New York: The Review of Reviews Company, 1918), pp. 468-70. Originally published by The Review of Reviews Company, 1917.

1. Open covenants of peace, openly arrived at....

2. Absolute freedom of navigation upon the seas....

3. The removal...of all economic barriers and the establishment of an equality of trade conditions among...nations....

4. ...national armaments will be reduced to the lowest point consistent with domestic safety.

5. ...impartial adjustment of all colonial claims....

6. ...evacuation of all Russian territory....

7. Belgium...must be evacuated and restored....

8. All French territory should be freed and the invaded portions restored....

9. A readjustment of the frontiers of Italy....

10. The peoples of Austria-Hungary...should be accorded the freest opportunity of autonomous development.

11. Rumania, Serbia, and Montenegro should be evacuated....

12. The Turkish portions of the present Ottoman Empire should be assured a secure sovereignty, but the other nationalities which are now under Turkish rule should be assured an undoubted security of life and...unmolested opportunity of autonomous development....

13. An independent Polish state should be erected....

14. A general association of nations [League of Nations] must be formed under specific covenants for...affording mutual guarantees of political independence and territorial integrity to great and small states alike.

Wilson tries to get Senate to go for League of Nations
(Punch, *London*)

Opposition to the Fourteen Points

Descended from an old Massachusetts family which had distinguished it-self in service to state and nation, Henry Cabot Lodge, a Republican, had become one of Woodrow Wilson's most inveterate foes long before the out-break of war. It was of little surprise, then, that Lodge would emerge as leader in the Senate's opposition to the Treaty of Versailles and to the League of Nations. In the aftermath of war Lodge shared the concern of the "Irreconcilables" with future American involvement in world affairs. In the following account, Lodge discusses his willingness to promote world peace, but he also makes clear his hesitancy involving further American global commit-ment, which, he feared, might lead to future hostilities.

Source: Henry Cabot Lodge, *The Senate and the League of Nations* (New York: Charles Scribner's Sons, 1925), pp. 407-09.

...We have not reached the great position from which we were able to come down into the field of battle and help to save the world from tyranny by being guided by others. Our vast power has all been built up and gathered by ourselves alone. We forced our way upward from the days of the Revolution, through a world often hostile and always indifferent. We owe no debt to anyone except to France in that Revolu-tion, and those policies and those rights on which our power has been founded should never be lessened or weakened. It will be no service to the world to do so and it will be of intolerable injury to the United States. We will do our share. We are ready and anxious to help in all ways to preserve the world's peace. But we can do it best by not crip-pling ourselves.

I am as anxious as any other human being can be to have the United States render every possible service to the civilization and the peace of mankind, but I am certain that we can do it best by not putting our-selves in leading strings or subjecting our policies and our sovereignty to other nations. The independence of the United States is not only more precious to ourselves but to the world than any single posses-sion. Look at the United States today. We have made mistakes in the past. We have had shortcomings. We shall make mistakes in the future and fall short of our own best hopes. But none the less is there any country today on the face of the earth which can compare with this in ordered liberty, in peace, and in the largest freedom? I feel that I can say this without being accused of undue boastfulness, for it is the simple fact, and in making this treaty and on these obligations all that we do is in a spirit of unselfishness and in a desire for the good of mankind. But it is well to remember that we are dealing with nations every one of which has a direct individual interest to serve and there is grave danger in an unshared idealism. Contrast the United States with any country on the face of the earth today and ask yourself whether the situation of the United States is not the best to be found. I will go as far as anyone in world service, but the first step to world service is the maintenance of the United States. You may call me selfish if you will, conservative or reactionary, or use any other harsh adjective you see fit to apply, but an American I was born, an American I have remained all my life. I can never be anything else but an American, and I must think of the United States first, and when I think of the United States first in an arrangement like this I am thinking of what is best of the world, for if the United States fails the best hopes of mankind fail with it. I have never had but one allegiance — I cannot divide it now. I have loved but one flag and I cannot share that devotion and give affection to the mongrel banner invented for a league. Internationalism, [refers to the unity of all workers throughout the world struggling against the forces of oppression] illustrated by the Bolshevik [a member of the Russian Communist Party] and by the men to whom all countries are alike provided they can make money out of them, is to me repulsive. National I must remain, and in that way I, like all other Americans, can render the amplest service to the world. The United States is the world's best hope, but if you fetter her in the interests and quarrels of other nations, if you tangle her in the intrigues of Europe, you will destroy her power for good and endanger her very existence. Leave her to march freely through the centuries to come as in the years that have gone. Strong, generous, and confident, she has nobly served mankind. Beware how you trifle with your marvelous inheritance, this great land of ordered liberty, for if we stumble and fall, freedom and civilization everywhere will go down in ruin.

"Teaching Him What To Say"
(Rollin Kirby in the New York World*)*

Deportation and the "Red Scare"

In the aftermath of war, many Americans came to believe that the country was beset by an internal threat from radical sources. The "Red Scare," as it came to be labeled, precipitated the Palmer Raids, named after Wilson's Attorney General, A. Mitchell Palmer, who, along with J. Edgar Hoover, played a significant role in masterminding the roundup of "radicals." The total dragnet — federal, state, and local — witnessed the arrest of thousands of immigrants, labor leaders, and political dissenters. What started as an attempt to defend American values and institutions from the criticisms of militant labor leaders, anarchists, Socialists, and Communists, ended as an assault upon the civil rights and liberties of countless innocent victims. When the furor was over, 249 people had been deported. Constantine Panunzio, an Italian immigrant and Methodist minister, undertook a study of those arrested for the Federal Council of Churches and uncovered blatant legal irregularities and abuses by American officials. In the following excerpt, Panunzio summarizes his findings.

Deportated "foreigners"
(National Archives)

Source: Constantine M. Panunzio, *The Deportation Cases of 1919-1920* (New York: The Federal Council of the Churches of Christ in America, 1921), pp. 93-97. Reprinted by DaCapo Press, 1970.

Personal History

We have found that these aliens were the common run of work-folk: store-keepers, shop-keepers, shoe-makers, carpenters, mechanics, unskilled laborers and the like. Nearly two-thirds of them were Russians. Almost nine-tenths were between the ages of 20 and 40. They had resided in this country for a comparatively long period. Over half of them had families, most of whom were living in the United States and included American-born children. The large majority had a little knowledge of English, and many of them had made application for American citizenship papers. A few had served in the United States military forces, and most of them had purchased bonds or in other ways taken part in war-time activities.

Arrests

We find that they were arrested mostly in groups while attending meetings in public halls. In not a few cases there were no warrants of arrest until long after the apprehension. At the police stations of other places of detention, a number of the aliens appear to have been forced to sign statements which were later introduced as evidence against them. It is also clear that at first they were not permitted to see their relatives or friends. Some evidently received cruel and abusive treatment at the time of arrest and during the period of detention.

Hearings

A "trial" was in some cases not given them until weeks after they were imprisoned. Even at best their "trial" was, provided by law, only an administrative hearing. In this proceeding the Immigrant Inspector, who was unusually a man untrained in law and often without even an academic training, acted as prosecutor, judge and jury at the same time. Interpreters were often necessary because the aliens' knowledge of English was so imperfect. In some instances the very man who originally had caused the arrest of the alien acted as interpreter at the hearing.

1918 Department of Labor poster, by Gerrit A. Beneker.
Its inscription reads: "The Past is Behind Us The Future is Ahead
Let us all strive to make the future better and brighter
than the past ever was."

Frequently the accused was not informed of his right to counsel, and when he was so informed, it was done after the representatives of the government had extracted from him, sometimes by inquisitorial methods, all the admissions they desired.

Alleged Radicalism

This cross-section study reveals that only a small number of these aliens could be classed as dangerous radicals. A large number of them were transferred from the Socialist Party either without their knowledge or without understanding the significance of such a transfer. We find evidence that aliens were induced to join proscribed organizations through the efforts of a provocative agent. The simplicity of their testimonies, of obvious sincerity, their straightforwardness, testify to the fact that the majority of the persons involved in this study were simple-minded folk who entertained no purpose hostile to the American Government or the American people. When questioned with reference to their desire to remain in this country most of them expressed not to be deported and said they would gladly abide by the laws of the United States....

Social Consequences

Some of the aliens were held for a considerable period, which was virtually equivalent to an indeterminate sentence. A number were detained for weeks after they had been ordered released. In the mean-time their families had been left without a means of support. As a consequence of all this a volume of prejudice and suspicion has been produced among immigrant groups, which it will require perhaps years to allay. It is impossible to know how much of the hostility now being reported on the part of foreign countries against America is due to the impressions made upon the nationals of other countries who have resided in the United States. It is difficult to avoid the conclusion that with the exception of the comparatively few persons who were clearly reportable under the law, these aliens needed not legal, but social and educational treatment looking toward an effectual integration to them of the best ideals of American life.

Historians and The Great War

Suffering from a stroke and rebuffed by the Senate over the Treaty of Versailles and his Fourteen Points, Wilson nonetheless proved to be prophetic. The failure to join the League and exercise American strength, reasons historian Arthur S. Link, paved the way for an unstable world order which soon permitted the emergence of dictators. By dismissing Wilson's warnings and refusing to participate in the efforts to establish a new world order, America helped prepare the way for these opportunists. In the final analysis, according to Link, Woodrow Wilson had played the role of prophet.

The Prophetic Vision of Woodrow Wilson

Source: Arthur S. Link, *Woodrow Wilson: Revolution, War, and Peace* (Arlington Heights, IL: Harlan Davidson, 1979), pp. 126-28. Originally published by The Johns Hopkins Press, 1957, under the title *Wilson the Diplomatist: A Look at His Major Foreign Policies.*

Meanwhile, the parliamentary phase of the struggle moved to its inexorable conclusion when the Senate took its second and final vote on the Treaty on March 19, 1920. The only hope for approval lay in the chance that enough Democrats would defy Wilson, as many friends of the League were urging them to do, to obtain a two-thirds majority for the Lodge reservations. Twenty-one Democrats did follow their consciences rather than the command from the White House, but not enough of them defected to put the Treaty across. The Treaty with the Lodge reservations failed by seven votes.

In this, the last and greatest effort of his life, did Wilson spurn the role of statesman for that of prophet? It is easy enough from our vantage point to say that, in rejecting ratification on the only possible terms and in throwing the issue into the party arena, he did not act as a statesman. It is also clear that his illness gravely impaired his perceptions of political reality and was probably the principal cause of his strategic errors.

However, when we view the situation through Wilson's eyes, his behavior seems neither irrational nor quixotic. As has been said many times, he believed that he had the overwhelming support of the American people. He was confident that he, or another pro-League Democrat, could do so again in 1920.

His friends feared that he would be devastated by Harding's victory. On the contrary, he was serene and confident on the morning after the election. He told his private secretary, "The Republicans have committed suicide." To the end of his life he was confident of the ultimate outcome and of the rectitude of his own position. As he put it: "I would rather fail in a cause that will ultimately triumph than triumph in a cause that will ultimately fail."

Wilson was fundamentally right in the one great principle at stake in the Treaty fight. The most immoral thing that a nation (or individual) can do is to refuse to exercise power responsibly when it possesses it. The United States exercised the greatest economic and potentially the greatest military power in the world in 1920. At least for a time it spurned the responsibility that accompanied its power.

Moreover, Wilson was fundamentally right in the long run. As he put it in a speech on Armistice Day in 1923: "We shall inevitably be forced by the moral obligations of freedom and honor to retrieve that fatal error and assume once more the role of courage, self-respect, and helpfulness which every true American must wish to regard as our natural part in the affairs of the world."

The postwar version of collective security failed in the crucial tests of the 1930s, not because the Treaty of Versailles was responsible or the peacekeeping machinery of the League of Nations was defective, but because the people of Great Britain, France, and the United States were unwilling to confront aggressors with the threat of war. Consequently, a second and more terrible world conflict came in 1939, as Wilson had prophesied it would.

The American people, and other peoples, learned the lesson that Wilson taught in 1919 and 1920, but at a fearful cost. And it is Wilson the prophet and pivot of the twentieth century who survives in history, in the hopes and aspirations of mankind for a peaceful world, and in whatever ideals of international service that the American people still cherish.

Allies celebrate their victory. (Army photo)

The Loss of Innocence

In one of the most illuminating analyses of the era, historian Henry F. May sees The Great War period as a time where the nation lost its innocence. The war disturbed the tranquility and optimism of Progressive America with its flurry of social, economic, and political activity and brought Americans face-to-face with the burdens of world power and demanding statesmen. With this change, according to May, the era can be seen as a watershed in American diplomatic history. In the following excerpt, May discusses America's "loss of innocence."

Source: Henry F. May, *The End of American Innocence: A Study of the First Years of Our Own Time, 1912-1917* (Chicago: Quadrangle Books, 1964), pp. 393-94, 398. Originally published by Alfred A. Knopf, 1959.

The war and its emotions passed with extraordinary suddenness. To see the full meaning of the story that ended in 1917 it is necessary to look beyond the wartime enthusiasm and beyond the complementary, savage disillusion of the postwar years. At some time long after the Armistice whistles had stopped blowing, it became apparent that a profound change had taken place in American civilization, a change that affected all the contenders in the prewar cultural strife. This was the end of American innocence. Innocence, the absence of guilt and doubt and the complexity that goes with them, had been the common characteristic of the older culture and its custodians, of most of the progressives, most of the relativists and social scientists, and of the young leaders of the prewar Rebellion. This innocence had often been rather precariously maintained. Many had glimpsed a world whose central meaning was neither clear nor cheerful, but very few had come to live in such a world as a matter of course....

....

Progress, right after the war, seemed to be equally shattered, and various types of reaction, long present beneath the surface, thrust militantly into the open. Racial violence reached an all-time high; the Fundamentalists made their most extreme and pathetic efforts to crush the liberalism which had seemed to them oppressive. A little later, in the mid-twenties, something else which had been latent before the war reached a position of great power: the ultra-practical, anti-intellectual, pseudoidealistic gospel of Prosperity First.

The end of American innocence was part of a great tragedy, but it was not, in itself, an unmitigated disaster. Those who look at it with dismay, or those who deny that it happened, do so because they expect true stories to have a completely happy ending. This is a kind of innocence American history must get over.

The Red Scare

In the postwar years the nation struggled to convert from a wartime to a peacetime economy. Unparalleled inflation, a surge of labor unrest, the cancellation of war contracts which triggered massive layoffs, all left the country perplexed. Into this mix came the "Red Scare." With the successful Bolshevik revolution in November of 1917 and the emergence of not one, but two Communist parties in the United States in the postwar period, fears were heightened by what many came to believe was an internal threat to the American way of life from social and political dissenters. In the following selection historian Robert K. Murray sees the concern with "Reds" as an episode of national hysteria that gripped Americans in the turmoil of the postwar years.

Source: Robert K. Murray, *Red Scare: A Study in National Hysteria* (Minneapolis: University of Minnesota Press, 1955), pp. 14-16.

In spite of the nation's desire for a rapid return to peace, it was obvious the American public of 1919 was still thinking with the mind of a people at war. Many prosecutions, already begun...were just coming before the courts and served to remind the nation of the existence of disloyalty. Returning soldiers, evidencing an intense love of country, added to the excitement by howling for the immediate and summary punishment of all such nonconformity. To the 1919 public the German was still a barbarian capable of committing any atrocity, while those who had sympathized with him or who had even slightly opposed the war were equally depraved. Indeed, anyone who spoke with an accent or carried a foreign name, German or otherwise, remained particularly suspect as American super-patriots continued to see spies lurking behind every bush and tree. Still in existence were the National Security League, the American Defense Society, and other such patriotic organizations which in order to live now sought to create new menaces. In short, insofar as the 1919 social mood was concerned the nation was still at war.

It was in the midst of this confusing, intolerant, and irresponsible atmosphere that the Great Red Scare occurred. The taproots of this phenomenon lay embedded in the various events growing out of the Bolshevik Revolution of November 1917. Denying most of the principles that older governments had been founded to secure and advancing the idea of worldwide proletarian revolution, the Bolshevik experiment was destined from the very beginning to represent one of the most crucial problems facing the world both during and after the war.

From the beginning the American public was shocked by the Bolsheviks disregard for the traditional and considered their separate peace with Germany a great betrayal. The nation then watched apprehensively as the Red Scourge moved westward into Europe. Patriotic societies, meanwhile, consistently denounced the Bolshevik as a counterpart of the dreaded Hun, and the press circulated much exaggerated information about the Bolshevik rein in Russia. Naturally, economic conservatism eagerly seized upon bolshevism's dangers in order to further their own campaign of stifling political and economic liberalism. The net result was the implantation of the Bolshevik in the American mind as the epitome of all that was evil.

On the other hand, great sympathy was immediately forthcoming from many American radicals for the Russian revolution and some openly advocated a similar upheaval in this country. In September 1919 two domestic Communist parties were formed, and while the movement remained very small, its noise more than compensated for its size. These American Communists held parades and meetings, dis-

tributed leaflets and other incendiary literature, and issued revolution-
ary manifestoes and calls for action.

In an intolerant postwar year in which people were still conditioned
to the danger of spies and sabotage, these domestic Bolsheviki seemed
particularly dangerous. As labor unrest increased and the nation was
treated to such abnormal events as general strikes, riots, and the planting
of bombs, the assumption that the country was under serious attack
by the Reds found a wide acceptance. In the long run, each social and
industrial disturbance was received as prima-facie evidence of the successful spread of radicalism. Even the temporary instability arising
from demobilization and reconversion, and the many justified protests
concerning high prices, were traced to the Reds.

As a result, exaggerated conclusions were reached concerning the
size and influence of the movement. Indeed, never before had the nation
been so overwhelmed with fear. It is understandable. Because of its
waning faith, its political and moral irresponsibility, and its momen-
tary abandonment of high ideals, the nation had been susceptible as
never before. Harassed by the ratings and ravings of a small group of
radicals, rebuffed by the dire warnings of business and employer organizations, and assaulted daily by the scare propaganda of the patriotic
societies and the general press, the national mind ultimately succumbed
to hysteria.

Suggestions for Further Reading

In addition to the works cited in the text, the following books are recommended:

Brooman, Josh, ed. *Great War: The First World War, 1914-1918.* White Plains, New York: Longman, 1985.

Bosco, Peter. *World War I.* New York: Facts on File, 1991.

" 'Clear and Present Danger' at Home During World War I," *Bill of Rights in Action.* vol. 4, Winter 1988, pp. 5-7.

Hawley, Ellis W. *The Great War and the Search for a Modern America.* New York: St. Martin's Press, 1992.

Hemingway, Ernest. *A Farewell to Arms.* New York: Charles Scribner's Sons, 1957, originally published by Charles Scribner's Sons, 1929.

Humble, Richard. *World War I Battleship.* New York: Franklin Watts, 1989.

Kennedy, David. *Over Here: The First World War and American Society.* New York: Oxford University Press, 1980.

Matthews, Rupert. *Attack on the* Lusitania. New York: Franklin Watts, 1989.

Maynard, Christopher and David Jeffris. *The Aces: Pilots and Planes of World War I.* New York: Franklin Watts, 1987.

Murphy, Paul L. *World War I and the Origin of Civil Liberties in the United States.* New York: W. W. Norton & Company, 1979.

Remarque, Erich Maria. *All Quiet on the Western Front,* Translated by A. W. Wheen. New York: Fawcett Crest, 1975. (Fiction. Originally published in book form in Germany in 1929 as *Im Westen nichts Neues.*)

Ross, Stewart. *War in the Trenches. World War I.* New York: Franklin Watts, 1991.

Stallings, Laurence. *The Doughboys.* New York: Harper & Row Publishers, 1963.

Trumbo, Dalton. *Johnny Got His Gun.* New York: Bantam Books, 1989. (Fiction)

Tuchman, Barbara. *The Zimmermann Telegram.* New York: The Macmillan Press, 1966.

About the Editor

A. J. Scopino, Jr., teaches history at Captain Nathan Hale Middle School in Coventry, Connecticut and Central Connecticut State University. He received an AB degree in history at St. Francis College, an AM in history at Brown University, and a Ph.D. in American history from the University of Connecticut. He is an expert on the American religious experience, centering on American pluralism and diversity. In addition to other writing, Dr. Scopino is also the editor of *The Progressive Movement: 1900 to 1917* in this series.